YOU'RE RICHER THAN YOU THINK

Grace Pathway Milestone 2.2

BILL GIOVANNETTI

Endurant Press

ISBN Ebook edition: 978-1-946654-11-3

ISBN Print edition: 978-1-946654-10-6

For additional resources, please visit maxgrace.com.

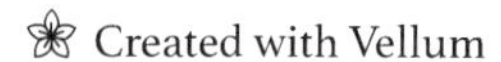

CONTENTS

NEW LABELS

Who are you?

It's an important question.

People act out of who they are.

Actually, people act out of who they *think* they are. Your identity determines your actions. Even if you promise yourself to start a new habit, no matter how strong your intentions, you're going to slip right back into your old habits as soon as the coffee wears off.

Or as soon as the baby starts crying, or somebody presses your buttons.

Why are we like this?

— BECAUSE THE LABELS WE ACCEPT CREATE SELF-FULFILLING PROPHECIES.

That's why one of the first things God wants us to understand is how HE sees us, and what beautiful labels he has put on our lives now that we have Jesus.

This little booklet is about the labels plastered on your soul.

COLLECTING LABELS

For all of our lives, we collect labels. Some are good, but, if you're like most people, a lot of those labels are not so good. Some are demeaning. A lot of them are painful.

Bullies and mean girls and stoned-out parents and uncaring teachers can slap labels on you that stick for a long time:

> *You are ugly, stupid, fat, skinny, a nerd, different, a loser, damaged goods, unwanted, unlovable, weak, impotent, unimportant, shy, awkward, evil, unlucky, cursed, doomed, pimply, a play toy, a slave, evil, trashy, defaced, a cripple, damned...*

Those labels worm their way into our hearts. They affect our lives for a very long time. They create self-fulfilling prophecies. If I call myself stupid long enough, I'm going to do a lot of stupid things.

I've had some of those labels plastered on my soul too. They twisted my sense of self. They distorted my identity. They made me so insecure, that I couldn't bring myself to say that I was going to be a pastor until very late in my (seven year) college program. The labels affected my relationships and life and even my money.

But one day, I learned a wonderful truth about my salvation. On the day that Jesus saved me, he peeled off every single one of those demeaning labels. He ran them through the shredder of his Calvary Love. And he blew the shreds away into powdery nothingness.

That is an awesome discovery... but wait, there's more!

NEW LABELS

Jesus didn't stop with peeling off all the painful labels in my life. He went farther. Jesus put new labels on me. Beautiful labels. Life giving labels. The old labels are gone! Only the new labels remain!

All those labels of doom and defeat were blasted to bits in the flood of Calvary's love. When Jesus Christ died on the cross, he stripped away once for all every demeaning label ever slapped on you by any demented foe. The mean girls have nothing to say to you. The bullies can no longer define you. The stoned out parents and absentee loved ones don't own your emotions. You don't need to spend one nano-second proving yourself to anybody. Your worth has been settled once for all. God has folded you into his family of faith forever, and has shouted to the heavens, "You are my beautiful child and, in you, I am well-pleased."

> Therefore, if anyone *is* in Christ, *he is* a new creation; old things have passed away; behold, all things have become new. (2 Corinthians 5:17)

If God says I am a new person, who am I to argue? This was an awesome discovery for me, and I'm hoping and praying you can experience the same amazing truth!

You can wake up every morning and declare the wonderful truth about yourself:

> *I am a new creation! I have a new name! I have new labels! You're looking at the new me! I am not who I used to be. I*

am who God says I am no matter what anybody else thinks!

These new labels run deeper than you think, and here's why.

JOINED TO JESUS

When God saved you, God joined you to Jesus. You became one with him. That was one of the ideas that getting baptized illustrates. Just as you are plunged into water physically, so you are plunged into Jesus, spiritually.

The Bible uses a little two word phrase to talk about our union with Christ. It uses the phrase, "In Christ." To be "in Christ" is to be one with him.

We have already seen this little phrase: If anyone is "in Christ," they are a new creation...

You are one with Jesus. You have been attached to him. You have been Super-glued to him. Stuck to him forever and ever with no possibility of ever coming unattached.

Here's where it gets good:

> — YOU ARE SO JOINED TO JESUS, THAT EVERYTHING THAT IS TRUE ABOUT JESUS IS NOW TRUE ABOUT YOU.

Everything you can say about Jesus, in his exalted humanity before God, you can also say about yourself.

Translation: *God puts on you the exact same labels he puts on Jesus Christ!!!!*

(I made the editor leave those exclamation points there.)

How do you think God labels Jesus? Accepted, beloved, beautiful, cherished, wanted... on and on it goes.

> *The astounding truth of being a Christian is that God puts on you the exact same labels that he puts on Jesus.*

If God says you are beautiful, who can argue? If he says you are acceptable in his sight, who cares what the mean girls say? If God declares you forgiven, you don't have to listen to the devil when he accuses you of guilt and shame even one second longer.

You have new labels.

You have new privileges.

You have a new identity.

You have new powers.

All of these labels and privileges and identity and powers are known as "your riches in Christ."

> Now we have received, not the spirit of the world, but the Spirit who is from God, that we might know *the things that have been freely given to us by God.* (1 Corinthians 2:12, emphasis added)

Think of that: God gave you himself (his Holy Spirit) to help you know "the things that have been freely given to us by God." I am writing to help you know your riches in Christ. I want you to know that becoming a Christian means you are richer than you think.

You are rich in who you are.

You are rich in whose you are.

You are rich in blessings.

You are rich in your destiny.

You are rich in your privileges.

You are rich in your exalted status in heaven as a royal child of God.

The rest of this booklet will get you started in understanding who you are and what you have now that you belong to God.

Here is just a sampling of your riches in Christ.

I AM ACCEPTED

To the praise of the glory of His grace, by which He has made us accepted in the Beloved. (Ephesians 1:6)

No human spirit thrives without a deep sense of acceptance. This represents a huge problem for a broken-down race, addicted to looking for love in all the wrong places. God designed the *family* as the fountainhead of acceptance and approval. Mom and Dad, when fulfilling their God-given design, fuel their children's gas tank with acceptance to last a lifetime.

That's the ideal.

Sadly, most of us run on fumes.

If you've ever struggled with self-acceptance, there is beautiful hope for you. Your Heavenly Father reaches out to you with an acceptance that knows no bounds. He loves you as he loves Christ, and he approves of you to the same measure.

He not only loves you, he likes you. He enjoys you. He values your company.

The Bible says you are "accepted in the Beloved"

(Ephesians 1:6). The Beloved is capitalized because it refers to the Beloved One, Jesus Christ.

In the Beloved One, because of your union with him, God accepts you just as much as he accepts Jesus. You are beloved in his sight, just like Jesus.

Any voices telling you the opposite are liars. Don't believe them. Don't listen to them. Don't curl up in a corner with Mr. Booze and indulge in a pity party. By the Word of God and the Spirit of God, you can silence the accusing voices ever-ready to trash your worth.

When the prodigal son came home, the father ran to him and smothered him with kisses. Whether you've been prodigal much or not, that is God's response as often as you turn to him in faith.

— YOU ARE BEAUTIFUL IN HIS EYES.

The biblical word translated "accepted" in Ephesians 1:6, sparkles with extra grace. One dictionary offers these definitions: "To make graceful, charming, lovely, agreeable. To pursue with grace, compass with favor. To honor with blessings." I am blown away to think that God pursues me with grace and compasses me with favor.

Disney has made a fortune telling stories of children desperately seeking their father's approval – think *Mary Poppins, The Sound of Music, Angels in the Outfield* (the remake), and *The Little Mermaid.*

May it comfort you to know, in good times and bad – whether you're on fire for God, or lukewarm before him, whether your behavior is decent or indecent – your truest Father approves of YOU, just as you are, in Christ. He delights in YOU. Even if your behavior is not so hot.

The next time you're tempted to berate yourself, reject yourself, or otherwise beat yourself up, let this beautiful reality crack through the crust of your self-rejection:

> The LORD your God in your midst, The Mighty One, will save; He will rejoice over you with gladness, He will quiet you with His love, He will rejoice over you with singing." (Zephaniah 3:17)

ADDITIONAL SCRIPTURES

Luke 15:23,24, Zephaniah 3:17, Isaiah 62:4.

MEDITATION

When God accepts a sinner, He is, in fact, only accepting Christ. He looks into the sinner's eyes, and He sees His own dear Son's image there, and He takes him in. ~Charles H. Spurgeon, 1800s

PRAYER

Dear Lord,

To think that you accept me as you accept Christ sometimes feels too good to be true. But it is true because you have said so. Today, I rest in this great reality. I bring my self-rejection to the foot of the Cross. I leave it there. I bring my performance anxieties, drives to achieve, obsessions over how I look, talk, act, and sound – Father, I lay them down at the Cross.

I lay my guilt and shame there too.

Lord, teach me to live with nothing left to prove.

I rest my soul in your perfect acceptance of me in Christ. I

move into your embrace. I look for my worth in my Savior – he is all I need.

As often as the voices of accusation rise up in my head, O Lord, silence them with the voice of your Word.

As often as feelings of condemnation well up in my heart, O Lord, transform them by the power of your love.

When nobody accepts me, I know you accept me still. This is all the confidence I need to face my day. I am rich because I am accepted by You.

By your grace, and for your glory,

Amen.

I AM ADOPTED

> For you did not receive the spirit of bondage again to fear, but you received the Spirit of adoption by whom we cry out, "Abba, Father." (Romans 8:15)

Your union with Christ joined you to the family of God – you share Christ's wonderful family status as a child of God. You are his son or daughter in faith's bloodline.

You may have grown up in a wildly dysfunctional family. Insanity, like fleas, hopped from person to person in your crazy family tree. You may look back on a long line of addicts, criminals, and abusers. Snooty religionists. Arrogant rebels.

No matter what your family of origin was like, God has given you a new family. Yes, we all bring our dysfunctions to the table, but the Father's wholesomeness is more than enough to counteract your kinfolk's craziness. Your Heavenly Father easily delivers his finest blessings behind the iron curtain of earthly dysfunction.

In what many would find the most meaningful reality

ever uttered about God, the Bible calls him "a father of the fatherless" (Psalm 68:5). Think about how awesome this is!

— GOD PROMISES TO FILL IN THE GAPS LEFT BY OUR IMPERFECT EARTHLY PARENTS.

Emotional gaps. Spiritual gaps. Even physical and financial gaps. God will move heaven and earth to prove to you that "father" is a verb, as he works tirelessly to unravel the painful knots tied by the failings of your earthly parents.

God is your Father in the best, most ideal sense possible. Whatever crud has accumulated over your father-concept – maybe your dad let you down or even hurt you – does not apply to God. Not even one little bit. Your truest Father loves you with a perfect love. You are the apple of his eye. He delights to call you his own.

God invites you to call him "Abba," which means Daddy.

- *He is a Father who provides for you.* "Or what man is there among you who, if his son asks for bread, will give him a stone?" (Matthew 7:9).
- *He is a Father who protects you.* "He shall cover you with His feathers, / And under His wings you shall take refuge; / His truth shall be your shield and buckler" (Psalm 91:4).
- *He is a Father who notices you.* "But the very

hairs of your head are all numbered" (Matthew 10:30).
- *He is a Father who exalts you* – he wears out the angels bragging about how awesome you are. "For to which of the angels did He ever say: 'You are My Son, Today I have begotten You'?" (Hebrews 1:5).
- *He is a Father who stays with you* – abandonment is not in his vocabulary. "...He will be with you, He will not leave you nor forsake you; do not fear nor be dismayed" (Deuteronomy 31:8).
- *He is a Father who glorifies you.* Your whole life story traces His plan to heap an avalanche of honor, glory, and celestial blessings on you some day. He is "bringing many sons [and daughters] to glory" (Hebrews 2:10).

You have been placed as an adult son or daughter into the royal family of God. His love for you equals his love for Christ. He approves of you. No frown of criticism ever creases his face. He looks upon you with joy. His name is your name. His wealth is your wealth. And his love is your love.

Your Father delights in you, and can hardly wait to welcome you home.

ADDITIONAL SCRIPTURES

Proverbs 3:12, Galatians 4:5-7, John 1:12, Galatians 3:26.

MEDITATION

Adoption is that act of God, whereby those were by nature the children of wrath, even as others, and were of the lost and ruined family of Adam, are from no reason in themselves, but entirely of the pure grace of God, translated out of the evil family of Satan, and brought actually and vitally into the family of God; so that they take his name, share the privileges of sons and they are to all intents and purposes the actual offspring and children of God. ~Charles H. Spurgeon, 1800s

PRAYER

My Gracious Father,

How I thank you for that glorious day you adopted me into your forever family. I was like an abandoned orphan wandering the streets, but you sought me out, and wrapped me up in your loving embrace. You made me your child forever.

Father. Abba. Daddy. I climb into your lap today. I rest in your love. I take my stand in the rights and privileges as a royal child of the Living God.

I calm my anxious heart in the knowledge of your ceaseless care. I profess to all the world your marvelous provision and presence.

I confess you as a father of the fatherless. I bless your name for the faithful ways you are filling up the gaps and healing the painful wounds left by my imperfect earthly parents. Lord, no matter how dysfunctional my earthly family has been, you have brought me into the most wholesome, whole, beautiful, and joyful family the cosmos has ever known.

Dad, take my hand, please, and walk me safely across this busy street called life-in-a-fallen-world. I'm already hungry for that glorious, raucous, joyful family dinner we will share someday in heaven's kitchen.

I am rich because I am adopted by You.

Through Jesus,

Amen.

I AM BLESSED

> Blessed be the God and Father of our Lord Jesus Christ, who has blessed us with every spiritual blessing in the heavenly places in Christ. (Ephesians 1:3)

There is no such thing as an unblessed Christian. If you are saved, you are blessed. Fully, richly, blessed. There's no stinginess with God's blessing. He drops down lavish boatloads of good stuff without measure and without price.

Most Christians make the soul-deadening mistake of coupling their daily moral performance with their level of blessing.

Nope.

You are blessed because Christ is blessed, and you are in him. He is the blessed Son of God. In him, you share his blessings. His blessings are your blessings.

Let's make sure we're clear on what the word *blessing* actually means. A blessing is a gift of grace. To bless is to give something good to someone no matter what they deserve.

God is not the heavenly boss, doling out paychecks for sweaty labor. God does not give paychecks; he gives blessings. He is not your employer; he is your Father. And he no more makes you work for your blessings than a loving father requires his toddlers to work for their Cheerios.

— GOD GIVES BLESSINGS, NOT PAYCHECKS.

And therefore, you don't serve God for blessings.

If you had to work for them, they couldn't be called blessings, by definition.

Do you realize what this means?

FREELY AND FULLY BLESSED

Quit working for blessings. Quit striving for blessings. Quit serving for blessings. Quit fasting, repenting, sweating, straining, and laboring for blessings.

The astounding fact of the gospel is God can't bless you any more than he has already blessed you. You are blessed because Christ is blessed, and you are "in him."

Let that sink in.

On the day you were saved, in that golden moment you first believed, God dropped on your head an avalanche of blessings. He put your name on a stellar portfolio of assets for every need, and every circumstance, and every opportunity you will ever face for all the rest of eternity.

You are mind-blowingly blessed beyond your wildest dreams, and it happened in the very first nano-second of your salvation, of your union with Christ.

Says who?

Says God: you have been "blessed with EVERY spiritual blessing in the heavenly places in Christ Jesus" (Ephesians 1:3). That is a past tense, completed act, for every child of God.

Peter affirms, "...His divine power has given to us all things that pertain to life and godliness..." (2 Peter 1:3). Notice the verb: *has given*, in the past tense. So this is a done deal. Notice what was given: *all things* that pertain to life and godliness. Not a few things. Not fifty percent. Not even ninety-nine percent, and then go chase down that last one percent.

No.

All things.

Paul asks the question every triumphant spirit already knows the answer to:

> He who did not spare His own Son, but delivered Him up for us all, how shall He not with Him also freely give us all things? (Romans 8:32)

How shall He not?

Answer: it's impossible to even conceive of it. To even imagine that the same generous God who was willing to give the astonishing gift of a beloved Son would suddenly grow stingy over a loaf of bread. How shall he not?

All things. There's your blessing.

If he gave you the hardest gift of all when he gave you Jesus, won't he with much more ease give you all the lesser gifts of life's relatively little blessings?

Let this promise flood your mind and heart: "And my

God shall supply all your need according to His riches in glory by Christ Jesus" (Philippians 4:19).

You can't not be blessed, because you are in Christ, and he is eternally blessed.

FEELING BLESSED

But you object: when the zombie apocalypse looms just over the horizon, and Dr. Jellyfinger offers nothing but bad news, how can you say I'm blessed? That's just crazy!

Let us now contemplate the difference between *being* blessed, which you are, and *feeling* blessed, which you might or might not be.

Just because you *are* blessed, it doesn't mean you *feel* blessed. Just because you are rich, it doesn't mean you feel rich. Just because you are loved, it doesn't mean you feel loved. Just because... well, point made.

The day after you're saved, you're still the same person you were the day before you were saved, but with one very huge difference: you are a new creation, identity-wise.

But you probably don't feel that way. You still have memories of your pre-saved days. You still have habits. Maybe there's a long list of lies you believe. Maybe your whole worldview has been pieced together by an army of little gollums, or brats, or thugs, or spoiled little princesses, or judgmental, legalistic, self-righteous Pharisees.

Past programming haunts you as you head into your new life in Christ. That's the source of your defeated spirit, your perpetual victim-status, your addiction, your hardness, and the mother of all your dysfunctions. And even if you were saved in childhood, you still swim every day in a sea of spiritual monsters. There's no way to live in this world without contracting the grime of depravity.

Even so...

- You are a new CREATION.
- But you are still living with old IDEATION.
- So what do you need most?
- You need TRANSFORMATION, BY THE RENEWING OF YOUR MIND (Romans 12:2).

That's the only way your *feelings* will ever catch up to the *truth* God says about you in Christ.

There's a beautiful prayer in the Old Testament, offered by a royally messed up King David, after the most heinous sin of his erratic life: "restore unto me the joy of your salvation" (Psalm 51:12). He doesn't pray for a restored salvation, because salvation is impossible to lose.

He prays for restored joy. He prays, not for blessing, but for the feeling of being blessed.

The gospel of God does not send you forth on a lifelong errand to *earn* your blessings.

— THE GOSPEL SENDS YOU FORTH TO BELIEVE IN THE BLESSINGS THAT BECAME YOURS ONCE FOR ALL IN THE HOUR YOU FIRST BELIEVED.

Write this down, make a poster, set it as your laptop's wallpaper, tattoo it across your soul, if not your forearm:

You don't serve God for blessing; you serve God from blessing.

If you could fly up to heaven right now, you'd see a huge pile of beautifully wrapped gifts with your name on them. These gifts are your blessings. Long before you were born, God looked down the corridors of time. He previewed your life. He saw every need, every circumstance, every trial, and every opportunity you would face. He knew your joys before you lived them. Your sorrows, too. God knew.

But he did more than just know.

God also provided. He has pre-prepared absolutely perfect provision for every moment of your life yet to come. Whatever supply you need, it's there. Whatever health, whatever wealth, whatever ideas, whatever courage, whatever *whatever* you need has been pre-supplied, pre-packaged, and pre-arranged. This doesn't mean you'll always be healthy or wealthy, but it does mean you'll be rich in treasures money can't buy.

DON'T FALL FOR THE DEVIL'S LIES

The devil works overtime to convince you of a lie. He wants you to doubt God's blessings. Maybe God won't provide for you. Maybe he doesn't care. Maybe God isn't strong enough. Or maybe you're just too unworthy. After all, look at the mess you've made! God may bless other people, but not you.

So you think.

And so you would be wrong.

Study your Bible. You will find this counter-intuitive reality: God never has, and never will, bless you because you've made yourself worthy. He blesses you because you've been joined to the Worthy One, the Lord Jesus Christ, by faith. So discover your possessions in Christ.

Count your blessings; name them one by one if you have to. Lay hold of your riches in Christ.

There's a great story about pioneer missionary Hudson Taylor packing up his family to go to the unreached masses of mainland China. In an age before telephones and Internet, his friends warned him, "You will be forgotten in that dark land."

Taylor replied, "I have two children. I have no problem remembering when they must eat. I know when they are tired. I know when they need a pillow for their heads. I do not forget my children. If I, a poor earthly father, can never forget my children or their needs, neither will my Heavenly Father forget me. No, I will not be forgotten."

That is the testimony of a person who can say every single day, come hell or high water, "I am blessed."

ADDITIONAL SCRIPTURES

Philippians 4:19, Micah 7:7, Psalm 23, 2 Corinthians 9:8.

MEDITATION

It is a wonderful thing to be really one with a risen and exalted Savior, to be a member of Christ! Think what it involves. Can Christ be rich and I poor? ~Hudson Taylor, 1800s

PRAYER

Gracious Father,

I acknowledge today you have blessed me better than I deserved. Not only that, you have blessed me to the full. You

have granted every spiritual blessing, and all things that pertain to life and godliness. All things are mine in Christ.

I am blessed because I am in Christ.

You know, Lord, the many times I have tried to buy a blessing from you. But today I won't do that, because your blessings aren't for sale. They are the blood-bought gifts of my Savior's perfect grace. I could never afford them, not in a million years of works and a million acts of contrition.

So I am blessed because Christ is blessed and I am one with him.

Thank you for such magnificent blessings. Thank you for a supernatural portfolio of everyday assets. Thank you for knowing my need and meeting it too. You are perfect in this. You have never let me down. I bless the God who has blessed my life.

I ask you, Lord, to restore to me the joy of my salvation. Grow in me the faith to feel my blessings, to see them with my own eyes, and to rest in your perfect provision and love.

I reject a whiny spirit. I reject a heart of victimization and despair. I will not live out of a sense of deficit today.

Instead, I will rest my soul in your overflowing love.

In this world so full of darkness, let me shine the light of a God-blessed life. Let others see your good hand upon me. And may they then turn, that they may find in you, the treasure that I have found because I found the Lord.

I am rich because I am blessed by You.

In Christ's Matchless Grace,

Amen.

I HAVE ACCESS

> Through whom also we have access by faith into this grace in which we stand, and rejoice in hope of the glory of God. (Romans 5:2)

My dad, Roy – now in heaven – grew up in Chicago loving baseball, especially the Chicago Cubs. As a kid, he routinely rode the bus to Wrigley Field where he could breathe the air of the "friendly confines." Once there, he'd join the pack of kids waiting on Waveland Avenue, behind left field. If a batter was strong enough, he could slam an out-of-the-park home run; it would land on Waveland with a huge bounce, and all the kids would scramble for the prize.

The biggest prize, however, was to score a ticket and get inside.

One lazy Sunday afternoon, young Roy had a thought. He eyed the walls separating himself from his beloved Cubs. The smell of popcorn and peanuts, the roar of the crowd inside, and the thought of ivy-covered walls were too much. He couldn't take being an outsider any more. So he did what any youthful, red-blooded baseball fan of that era would do: he started climbing the left-field wall. He scoped out a climbing path, and started climbing.

He made it about twelve feet above ground before he got busted.

A man in a suit called to him, my dad said, and made him climb down. Then that man told young Roy to come with him. Roy was scared. His mind ran scenarios of how his strict Italian parents would react. Roy thought of running, but the man had ushers with him. He thought of pleading, but the man looked too stern.

He walked along in silence, looking for any way out of his doom. His palms sweated. His heart pounded. The man walked my dad to the nearest entrance to Wrigley Field. He walked him through the gates, through the turnstiles, past the gatekeepers. Past security. His mind raced. Would they call the cops? On the way in, Roy heard the most magical words he could imagine: "Good afternoon, Mr. Wrigley."

That man in the suit – that man who called my dad down from his climbing and escorted him to his personal front row seats to enjoy the game – that man was Philip K. Wrigley, son of William Wrigley, whose gum you've probably chewed, and whose formerly hapless baseball team you've probably scorned.

The son brought my dad past the barrier and gave him access to his heart's deepest desires.

God's Son did the same for you.

That mountain of sin that barred you from God: removed.

That burden of debt that crushed your hopes: paid in full.

That wall of divine holiness, that fire of divine presence, that fear of infinite company: breached, quenched, resolved.

Whatever barrier stood between you and Heaven's Mighty God has been demolished and removed once and for all.

Through Christ's Cross, and now by virtue of union with him, you have an all-access pass to the heavenly realms. It's valid right now. Here on earth. Even before you die and go to heaven. You have access.

— YOU CAN APPROACH GOD ANYPLACE,
ANY TIME, FOR ANY REASON.

When you pray, you can be confident he is as near as your prayer's first breath.

You can approach him boldly. No groveling needed. God's children don't beg. They rise to their full stature before heaven's throne, state their needs, thank their Father, and get on with their day. Do not fear to approach your King. He is mighty to save, and loves your biggest requests.

I have this suspicion that when we finally see the Savior face to face, he won't berate us for bringing him prayers that were too big.

When you approach, approach him boldly, without fear. Come into his presence without the slightest doubt of his willing acceptance. He wants your company. He enjoys your conversation. He seeks you that you might seek him.

You can approach him immediately. You do not need to prep. You do not need to primp. No preliminaries needed. No reduction of sin. No improvement of your Ten Commandments batting average. No contrition over wrongs you have done. He says to come and to come boldly. So do it without hesitation. Come just as you are.

You can approach him directly. Do not attempt to reach him through intermediaries. You need no saint, no priest, no pastor, and no pope – not even Mary – to soften up God before you arrive.

You have an all-purpose Mediator in Christ, and he is the only one you need (1 Timothy 2:5).

How would you like it if your child always sent a few envoys ahead of lunch to find out your mood and to ask for extra fries? You'd know something was wrong in the relationship.

And so it is with God. You have 24/7 access to the King of kings and Lord of lords. He knows you personally. And he likes you.

Peel off any labels that make you feel like an unwelcome outsider. God labels you part of his innermost circle.

Believe it.

The heavenly security team is waiting for you – they've been briefed. They know your name. They won't stop you. The heavenly gates are opened for you. Walk through with a full assurance of faith. The heavenly table is set for you. Come and dine on the richest of fare. Access is yours. No barriers in sight.

Right now, Almighty God waits for you with eager anticipation.

What are you waiting for?

ADDITIONAL SCRIPTURES

Romans 5:2, Ephesians 2:18; 3;12, Hebrews 4:16.

MEDITATION

Do not live as if God were as far off from you as the east is from the west. Live not far below on the earth; but live on high, as if you were in heaven. In heaven you will be with God; but on earth He will be with you: is there much difference? ~Charles H. Spurgeon, 1800s

PRAYER

Gracious Father,

How I bless you for this tremendous access to the courts of heaven. The throne of grace is there for me, for your Son has opened the way. No angel will stop me and no demon can try. Not even the devil can bar me from you.

Yet sometimes, I hesitate. I think you're mad at me, or I delude myself into needless preliminaries. I'm sorry for that. But I profess today: my sins don't exclude me, my guilt can't blockade me, and nothing I can ever do or fail to do will shut me out from your holy presence.

So, Father, I draw near in full assurance of faith.

I come to you in my need. I come to you in my sorrows. I come to you in my joys. I come to you for everything and for nothing.

In your presence, I find peace in my problems, clarity in

my perplexity, and comfort in the dark night of my soul. I find the embrace of a Father, the familiarity of a friend, and safety of an advocate and protector.

I find rest for my soul.

All those things that worry me, I lay at your feet. I let them go. In your time, do your mighty work. I have access to heaven; what on earth can steal my joy?

I am rich because I have access to You.

In Christ I pray,

Amen

I AM FORGIVEN

Come now, and let us reason together," Says the Lord, Though your sins are like scarlet, They shall be as white as snow; Though they are red like crimson, They shall be as wool. (Isaiah 1:18)

This chapter on forgiveness is written by a guy whose middle name is "guilt trip." The little church that reared me blessed me beyond words; I'm thankful for that. But I'm also recovering from the painful labels of unworthiness and guilt slapped on me during those formative years.

Sometimes a church can feel like a travel agent for a guilt trip.

No matter how many prayers I prayed or good works I squeezed out, I was sure God was judging me for my sins. I cringed to think of standing in his presence. Even though I was saved, I still stooped beneath a hundred pound sack of guilt.

So I did what any self-respecting church kid would do: I made myself super-busy for Jesus. I served him all the time. If the church doors were open, I was there. But my service wasn't out of love; it was out of guilt. I didn't know it at the time, but my service was a form of penance, and I didn't even believe in penance.

Today, I can say with all belief that I am permanently, profoundly, and perfectly forgiven by God forever. This is not because God is wimpy, but because the Cross of Christ is strong.

What made the difference?

An understanding of the Cross and what happened for me the day Jesus died.

A FORGIVING GOD

The astounding announcement of the prophets and apostles of old is the good news of a forgiving God.

In Christ, you stand fully, completely, perfectly, everlastingly forgiven of all your sins, past, present and future. Even if you went out and invented a brand new sin – a big, juicy, heinous sin no one had ever done before – your forgiveness from God wouldn't even flicker.

This is not due to God's leniency, softness, niceness, or "unconditional" love. To reduce the biblically glorious wonder of forgiveness into a divine wimpiness, by which the Creator winks at sin, is to set yourself up for a lifetime of a troubled conscience.

We need a forgiveness that means something – a forgiveness so strong that a thousand shouts of devilish accusation can't shake it. And that is exactly what God has lavished upon us, courtesy of the Cross of Christ.

A HOLY GOD

Behind the Cross lies the initially uncomfortable, but ultimately beautiful, reality of an infinitely holy God. If God were not holy, Jesus would not have died.

The holiness of God implies two very scary truths for any thinking person:

The first is that sinful people cannot dwell in God's presence. If God is holy, anyone who has sinned stands alienated from him. In other words, if God is holy, you can't be his friend without measuring up to his standards. So the Bible says we are "alienated from the life of God," and, we were "alienated and enemies" of God "by wicked works" (Ephesians 4:18, Colossians 1:21).

This is horrible news.

But wait, there's more, and the second truth gets worse:

God's holiness also implies that sinful people fall under condemnation from the justice of God. It's not just that we're alienated from God; as sinners we're condemned by God, too. I know this feeds into a lot of negative stereotypes about God, but we do ourselves no favors by avoiding the difficult truth. God judges sin. The Bible says, "the wrath of God is revealed from heaven against all ungodliness and unrighteousness" of people (Romans 1:18). Jesus warned anyone who stood aloof from his way of forgiveness that "the wrath of God abides on him" (John 3:36). This wrath lasts forever (Matthew 25:46).

Far from being a grandmotherly leniency on the part of a God too wimpy to care, true forgiveness can be nothing less than a tough, rigorous, righteous action on the part of a frighteningly holy God.

THE NON-DILEMMA

"God is love," says John (1 John 4:8).

"Our God is a consuming fire," says Hebrews (12:29).

Do you see a problem here? God's love won't bless where his holiness is offended. From our standpoint, this looks like a dilemma. God, however, is too smart to ever have a dilemma. In his perfect plan, he made a way to love us without tossing his holiness into the dumpster.

Enter the Cross, where Jesus died. The crucifixion towers above history as a monument to both the fierce wrath and invincible love of God. Take away either, and the Cross makes no sense.

> — WHEN CHRIST WAS NAILED TO THE CROSS, YOUR SINS WERE NAILED TO CHRIST.

This is the lesson God had to teach me to deliver me from my load of guilt. I'll never forget the day. I sat in my musty high school gymnasium – in the same school that so tormented Susan – reading a book about the cross of Christ. Suddenly, the lights came on. I got it. It clicked. The Cross made sense to me. And that hundred pound sack of guilt dropped to the ground. In an instant I knew I was forgiven.

My sins were nailed to Christ, and he paid the price for them. Your sins were nailed to Christ and paid for too.

God reached into you – long before you were born – and collected all your sins. Every failure, every loss, every hatred, every lie, every immoral thought, every abuse, cruelty, and omission – every sin, past, present and future, God collected them all.

He then transferred your sins to Christ.

So the Bible says, Jesus "himself bore our sins in his own body" on the cross (1 Peter 2:24). "The Lord [God the Father] laid on him [God the Son] the iniquity of us all," said Isaiah (Isaiah 53:6).

Christ hung on that cross as if he had done your crimes, committed your sins, and failed your failures.

Then God did the unthinkable: he punished Christ for your sins instead of punishing you. The pent up Judgment Day against a world gone wild was unleashed against the bloodied Savior, hanging all alone, between heaven and earth. "Christ crucified" was the lightning rod that absorbed God's wrath that he might spare you. He died as your substitute.

He died horribly. Painfully. In utter agony. Forsaken and alone. We bow in humble adoration at the bloody crucifixion of our precious Savior.

Because of that death, God is free to dismiss your sins from his presence. He sees no guilt in you – you stand faultless before him (Jude 24).

Because of what Christ did.

Not because of what you did. No, not even a tiny bit.

Don't you think Christ's sacrifice was enough? Is there anything you can add? Are there coins you might supply to sweeten the deal with God? Did Jesus accidentally leave a few sins behind for you to atone for?

Crazy-talk.

IT IS FINISHED

In his final breath, Jesus said, "It is finished" (John 19:30) – the best words ever uttered on planet earth. The payment for your sin was finished. The judgment of God against you was finished. Your guilt and shame were finished, once for all, on the cross, by Christ alone.

"Behold, the Lamb of God, who takes away the sin of the world" (John 1:29).

That is why you can say today, *I am forgiven* – totally, irrevocably, everlastingly, forgiven – for all my sins, past, present, and future. You possess a hard-fought, blood-bought, paid in full, comprehensive, once for all, perfectly legitimized, unassailable forgiveness from the heart of your magnificently holy God. You did not deserve it. You did not earn it. You can't contribute to it. You received it the day God joined you to Christ.

In Christ, God labels you FORGIVEN. He longs for you to label yourself FORGIVEN too.

ADDITIONAL SCRIPTURES

Psalm 103:10-12, Romans 8:1, Ephesians 1:7, John 8:1-11.

MEDITATION

We are now pardoned; even now are our sins put away; even now we stand in the sight of God accepted, as though we had never been guilty. "There is therefore now no condemnation to them which are in Christ Jesus." There is not a sin in the Book of God, even now, against one of His people. ~Charles H. Spurgeon, 1800s

PRAYER

Dear Lord,

I stand today in the forgiveness purchased by Jesus Christ on the cross. Thank you for such a sacrifice. By the Cross, you honored both your holiness and your love. Your forgiveness of me is just, holy, righteous, and pure. I stand free from guilt, free from shame, free from condemnation.

Thank you, God, for the Cross of Christ. Thank you for Calvary Love. I am humbled and grateful when I think of that great sacrifice. Such agony, such pain, such a death, for me. I bless you as my Savior. I worship you as my King. I find my shelter in the shadow of the cross, and know no sin can condemn me there.

I claim my forgiveness in Christ, today and everyday.

On the authority if Christ's Cross, I label myself FORGIVEN.

I may fail a thousand times today. I may let you down. I may let myself down.

But of this I am sure: you have forgiven me, once for all. You have cast my sins behind your back and dismissed them as far as the east is from the west. You have washed me in the blood of the Lamb.

I peel off the labels of guilt and shame. I peel off the labels of self-punishment. I peel off labels of penance. I rest my conscience at the foot of the cross. I tell the accusing voices in my head that your forgiveness of me is total, permanent, finished, and exhaustive. I command those voices to be silent. God has spoken. I am clean. I am forgiven. It is finished.

The only label I accept today when it comes to my sins is FORGIVEN. I am rich because I have forgiveness in You.

Through My Precious Savior I pray.

Amen.

WHAT'S NEXT

You are rich! You are rich in things that money can't buy!

I hope you have a great running start in discovering the treasure you have now that you belong to Jesus. There is a whole lot more just waiting for you!

You can also dig deep by learning how to read the Bible and pray — a daily habit that will change your world. That's the next booklet in the Grace Pathway!

I'm praying for you! Keep Growing!

There are three booklets in Milestone 2/God Blesses You.

- 2.1 — Secure Forever
- 2.2 — You're Richer Than You Think
- 2.3 — How to Have a Quiet Time

Now, it's time to learn how to fuel your heart with God's love every single day.

If you'd like to go deeper into the topic of your identity and labels in Christ, I have a written whole book about it called *Grace Rehab.* There is a companion workbook for group and personal reflection. You can unearth even more of your riches in Christ. You'll find this and other resources at:

www.maxgrace.com

Made in the USA
Middletown, DE
23 October 2024